CAITLIN CLARK:

A Shooting Star's Journey- Beyond the Buzzer

Caitlin clark

Elizabeth J. Williams

Caitlin clark

All Right reserved. No part of this publication may be reproduced, distributed or transmitted in any form or by any means, including photocopying, recording or other electronic or mechanical methods, without the prior written permission of the publisher, except in the case of brief quotations embodied in critical reviews and certain other noncommercial uses permitted by copyright law.

Copyright © Elizabeth J. Williams , 2023.

TABLE OF CONTENTS

INTRODUCTION

CHAPTER 1: WHO IS CAITLIN CLARK

1:1 Early life

1:2 Family background

CHAPTER 2: ATHLETIC JOURNEY

2:1 Introduction to basketball

2:2 Academic success in high school

2:3 College Recruitment Process

CHAPTER 3: COLLEGE CAREER

3:1 Choosing a college

3:2 Impacts on the team

CHAPTER 4: NOTABLE ACHIEVEMENTS

4:1 Awards

4:2 Recognitions

CHAPTER 5: PLAYING STYLE AND SKILLS

    5:1 Offensive prowess

    5:2 Defensive abilities

    5:3 Leadership on the Court

CHAPTER 6: CHALLENGE

    6:1 Triumphs

    6:2 Overcoming Adversity

6:3 Memorable Games and Moments
CHAPTER 7: OFF THE COURT
7:1 Academic pursuits
7:2 Community involvement
CHAPTER 8: LEGACY
8:1 Impacts
8:2 Women's Basketball Contributions

8:3 Influence on Future Generations
CHAPTER 9: RISING STAR STATUS
CONCLUSION

Caitlin clark

INTRODUCTION

One name sticks out like a shooting star across the night sky in the thrilling world of women's collegiate basketball: Caitlin Clark. In "Caitlin Clark: A Shooting Star's Journey Beyond the Buzzer," we go on an absorbing investigation into the unmatched talent, passion, and life that characterize one of the most fascinating characters in sports.

This book explores the incredible rise of Caitlin Clark, an extraordinary talent who changed the game forever on her way from the heartland of Des Moines, Iowa, to the national stage. Beyond the spectacular crossovers and buzzer-beating shots, we discover the layers of commitment, tenacity, and unadulterated talent that define Clark's rise to prominence.

Caitlin clark

Each chapter highlights a significant turning point in her development, from her early years on the neighborhood courts to her reign as the University of Iowa Hawkeyes' Queen. "A Shooting Star's Journey Beyond the Buzzer" presents a compelling picture of Caitlin Clark, not only as an incredible athlete but also as a resilient trailblazer who is redefining what's possible on the basketball court, through incisive anecdotes, behind-the-scenes revelations, and exclusive interviews.

Come along as we examine the highs and lows, victories and setbacks that have molded Caitlin Clark into the modern-day icon that she is. Readers will see the unwavering spirit that propels her past the buzzer and into the annals of basketball greatness through the lens of her incredible journey. Prepare to be amazed by Caitlin Clark's genius—a shooting star whose potential has no bounds.

CHAPTER 1: WHO IS CAITLIN CLARK

Caitlin Clark is an American basketball player born on June 19, 2001, in Des Moines, Iowa. She gained national recognition for her outstanding performance in women's college basketball.

For the University of Iowa Hawkeyes, Clark was a guard who had an immediate impact during her freshman year. She immediately established herself as one of the most fascinating and talked-about players in the NCAA thanks to her amazing scoring ability, three-point shooting prowess, and playmaking skills.

Caitlin Clark made a name for herself as one of the best high school athletes in the nation while attending Dowling Catholic in West Des Moines, Iowa. She won numerous awards and demonstrated her abilities on a national platform.

The influence of Caitlin Clark goes beyond the basketball floor. There is excitement for her future in

Caitlin clark

basketball due to her exceptional skill at scoring, passing the ball, and leading her team, which has led to comparisons with some of the greatest players in history.

During her first year at the University of Iowa (2020–2021), Clark won multiple awards, including the Big Ten Freshman of the Year title and the All-Big Ten First Team distinction. Her performances, which included triple-doubles and high-scoring games, were a major factor in the Iowa Hawkeyes' victory.

In addition to her sporting accomplishments, Clark has developed into an inspiration for aspiring athletes. Fans and colleagues alike have expressed admiration for her commitment to the game, work ethic, and leadership both on and off the court. Clark's influence extends beyond the numbers she racks up; she also serves as an inspiration to young athletes aspiring to be like her.

Caitlin Clark's story is far from over, but it promises more thrilling moments and contributions to the world of women's basketball as she advances through her college career and possibly moves on to the professional ranks.

1:1 Early life

On June 19, 2001, Caitlin Clark was born in Des Moines, Iowa, which marked the beginning of an incredible journey in the basketball world. Born and raised in the American Midwest, Clark's love for athletics was evident from a young age. Her first dribbles were performed on Des Moines neighborhood courts, displaying the raw skill that would eventually win over the basketball community.

It was clear even in those early years that Clark had a special bond with the game. Her skills were greatly cultivated by the support of her family, coaches, and the local basketball community. She started to distinguish herself as a young athlete not only for her innate ability but also for her work ethic and commitment to learning the nuances of the sport.

Caitlin clark

Caitlin Clark's early years established the groundwork for her extraordinary basketball journey. She had no idea that her early court experiences in Iowa would set the stage for a career filled with record breaks, honors, and a profound influence on the women's college basketball scene.

1:2 Family background

A stellar high school basketball career was part of Caitlin Clark's resume, which helped establish her as one of the country's best prospects. When she was a student at Dowling Catholic High School in West Des Moines, Iowa, people soon took notice of her abilities on the court. College basketball programs were eager to sign Clark because of her extraordinary scoring ability, court vision, and leadership traits.

Her impressive statistical performances and multiple accolades were part of her high school basketball accomplishments. Because of her skill on the court, Clark was named a McDonald's All-American and

Caitlin clark

participated in the Jordan Brand Classic, confirming her place among the nation's most promising players.

Caitlin Clark chose to play collegiate ball and made her commitment to the University of Iowa. She embraced the chance to have a big influence on the program, which gave her another dimension to her story when she decided to stay in her home state and play for the Iowa Hawkeyes.

CHAPTER 2: ATHLETIC JOURNEY

The athletic career of Caitlin Clark is an incredible story of perseverance and talent enhancement. She showed an innate talent for basketball at a young age, drawing the interest of peers and coaches alike. Her adventure started in neighborhood youth leagues, where her innate ability became apparent.

As Clark advanced through middle school, it was clear that she was dedicated to improving her abilities. Her enthusiasm for the game combined with her strong work ethic made her stand out in high school showcases. These early triumphs set the stage for a successful basketball career.

The hiring process in her senior year of high school demonstrated Clark's high demand as a candidate. Her leadership abilities, court vision, and scoring prowess were noticed by college scouts. An important turning

Caitlin clark

point in her journey was choosing which college to attend, which ultimately determined the course of her collegiate career.

Clark made a name for herself in college basketball very quickly. Her explosive style of play and dominance on the court attracted national attention. She was not only a standout individual but also a driving force behind the success of her team, demonstrating leadership abilities well beyond her years.

Clark encountered difficulties during her time in college that put her fortitude to the test. Whether they occurred on or off the court, these challenges turned into chances for development and education. Her handling of hardship demonstrated not only her physical prowess but also her resilience and willpower.

Significant junctures in Caitlin Clark's career were marked by memorable games and highlight-reel plays. Her legacy was enhanced by each accomplishment, which also cemented her place among the elite players in women's college basketball. Her dedication to education and community service outside of the court further demonstrated the all-encompassing mindset she brought to her athletic career.

Fans and aspiring athletes alike can find inspiration in Caitlin Clark's athletic journey as it unfolds. She has made a lasting impression on the sport and paved the way for what looks to be an exciting and significant career. Her influence goes beyond the box score.

2:1 Introduction to basketball

Caitlin Clark's fascination with basketball dates back to her early years. Her early experiences with the sport, whether it was dribbling a ball in the driveway or shooting baskets at the neighborhood park, kindled a passion that would accompany her throughout her journey. It became clear that basketball was more than just a hobby for Clark as she made the switch from

Caitlin clark

unorganized play to structured youth leagues: it was her calling.

The foundational abilities she developed during these early years prepared her for future success on the court. Clark's natural talent was noticed by mentors and coaches, and their dedication to seeing her progress became a motivating factor. She used the basketball court as a canvas to showcase her athletic expression, combining skill that had been developed with natural ability.

Her playing style was shaped by these early experiences, which also imparted resilience, discipline, and teamwork values. The path from pick-up basketball on the playground to competitive youth leagues set the stage for an incredible basketball career. Caitlin Clark had no idea how her early exposure to the sport would pave the way for an incredible journey and leave a lasting impression on the sport she would eventually come to love.

Caitlin clark

2:2 Academic success in high school

The accomplishments Caitlin Clark has achieved in high school bear witness to her extraordinary talent and commitment to the game of basketball. Not only did she win a lot of local competitions during her high school years, but her exceptional skills on the court also brought her national recognition.

1. Scoring Prowess: Clark was known for her outstanding point contributions in every game, constantly displaying an unmatched ability to score.
   - Her reputation as a prolific high school scorer was cemented by her high-scoring performances in pivotal games.

2. Acclaim and Awards: Received numerous honors, including Player of the Year and All-State recognition, establishing her as one of the area's best high school basketball players.

Caitlin clark

- Attained widespread recognition, as evidenced by nominations for major honors that emphasized her influence in high school basketball circles.

3. Team Leadership: Clark's impact as a team captain in high school went beyond her own accomplishments.
   - led her team to important wins while exhibiting the leadership traits that would later come to define her playing style.

4. Record-Breaking Performances: Set and broke multiple records in high school basketball, as well as state and, occasionally, national records.
   - Reached goals that demonstrated her extraordinary abilities and left a lasting impression on the high school basketball scene.

5. National Recognition and Exposure: Attracted the interest of college scouts and basketball enthusiasts nationwide by showcasing her talents in prestigious national tournaments and showcases.

- Relentlessly ranked among the nation's best high school athletes, enhancing her standing as a rising star in the basketball world.

In addition to laying the foundation for her college career, Caitlin Clark's high school accomplishments gave fans a sneak peek at the brilliance she would eventually experience as a college basketball player. Her influence during these early years created a lasting impression on the high school basketball scene and paved the way for an incredible future.

2:3 College Recruitment Process

The college recruiting process for Caitlin Clark was an extremely competitive and eagerly awaited stage of her basketball career. Being one of the most sought-after high school prospects, she was vying to join the teams of several elite college programs.

Caitlin clark

1. Scouting and Recognition: College recruiters and scouts started keeping a close eye on Clark's high school performances after realizing her extraordinary talent and potential impact on college campuses.

   Her visibility increased as a result of national rankings and awards, drawing interest from numerous college basketball programs.

2. Official Visits and Conversations: Clark made official visits to a number of colleges, which gave her the chance to see the campus, interact with the coaching staff, and determine how well each program fit her needs overall.

   - Talking with coaches about their expectations for her on their teams and the possibility of both personal and athletic growth was very important.

3. Decision-Making Process: Clark negotiated a difficult decision-making process to choose the college that best matched her objectives and aspirations by taking into account academic offerings, playing style, team dynamics, and personal preferences.

Caitlin clark

 - An additional degree of suspense surrounded the hiring process due to public curiosity and conjecture regarding her choice.

4. Proclamation and Promise: The much awaited announcement of the commitment turned into a significant occasion for supporters, teammates, and the collegiate basketball community.
 - After a careful evaluation process, Clark decided to commit to a specific university, which signified the start of her collegiate journey.

5. Impact on the Selected Program: Clark's dedication significantly improved the selected college program, raising awareness among supporters and elevating its stature right away. The program's visibility in the competitive landscape was enhanced by the recruitment success, which in turn raised expectations for her contributions to the team's success.

Caitlin clark

A fascinating chapter in Caitlin Clark's career, her college recruitment process demonstrated not only her athletic ability but also her ability to make calculated decisions and her influence in the world of college basketball. In the end, her decision paved the way for a college career that would enthrall basketball fans all over the country.

Caitlin clark

CHAPTER 3: COLLEGE CAREER

Caitlin Clark Has Had An Incredible College Career, Demonstrating Both Individual Talent And Major Team Contributions. Here's A Look At Her Memorable Collegiate Basketball Career So Far:

1. Freshman Impact: Clark Made An Instant Impression As A Freshman Thanks To Her Leadership, Court Vision, And Scoring Prowess. Her Plays Attracted National Notice, And She Soon Found Herself At The Center Of Conversations About Women's College Basketball.

2. Scoring Records And Milestones: Clark Continuously Demonstrated Her Scoring Prowess Throughout Her College Career, Shattering Records And Hitting Significant Scoring Thresholds.
   - Her Ability To Influence Results With Her Offensive Skills Was Demonstrated By Her High Point Totals In Games And Season Averages.

Caitlin clark

3. Versatility On The Court: Well-known For Her Adaptability, Clark Showed That She Could Influence The Game In A Number Of Ways, Including Rebounding, Playmaking, And Scoring. Because Of Her Explosive Playing Style, She Presented A Difficult Opponent To Match Up With And Became The Center Of Defensive Tactics.

4. Team Leadership: Accepting the role of leader, Clark led her group both on and off the court. Her impact went beyond the numbers, as she was essential in forming the success and culture of the team.

5. Awards and Recognitions: Received numerous honors and recognitions, such as conference honors, selection to the All-American team, and consideration for esteemed national awards.
   - Her influence on the collegiate basketball scene became widely recognized as a result of her continuous excellence.

Caitlin clark

6. Postseason Success: Clark's influence was especially noticeable in postseason play, as she improved in key situations.

 - added to her legacy by making a major contribution to her team's performance in NCAA March Madness and conference tournaments.

7. Legacy and Influence: Clark's influence grew outside the court as her collegiate career went on, motivating teammates and creating a lasting legacy within her college program. Her accomplishments attracted the respect of both fans and other athletes, elevating the profile of women's collegiate basketball.

Throughout her stellar college career, Caitlin Clark has established herself as one of the top players in women's collegiate basketball. In the world of collegiate athletics, her journey continues to be an inspirational tale as she makes headlines and helps her team succeed.

Caitlin clark

3:1 Choosing a college

Caitlin Clark carefully considered a number of factors before deciding on a college, all of which were significant influences on her college experience:

1. Academic Fit: Education-related offerings and programs were taken into account as a crucial component. Clark probably evaluated how well each university matched her intended field of study and educational objectives.

2. Basketball Program and Coaching Staff: An important consideration was the coaching staff's reputation as a whole as well as the style of play and philosophy of the program.

Talking with coaches about her possible position on the squad and the opportunities for growth gave her an idea of how she would advance as a player.

Caitlin clark

3. Team Dynamics and Culture: Clark found it critical to evaluate the dynamics and culture of the team. Her choice was probably impacted by a cohesive and encouraging team atmosphere, which affected her overall performance and experience on the court.

4. Facilities and Resources: Her decision would have been influenced by the caliber of the training tools, support systems, and athletic facilities, all of which would have aided in her athletic development.

5. Location and Campus Environment: The university's physical location as well as the general campus atmosphere probably had an impact. A consideration of community, lifestyle, and weather conditions would have affected her comfort and well-being.

6. Possibilities for Exposure: Clark's decision was probably impacted by her desire for recognition and her chance to compete at a high level. Choosing a college with a potent basketball program would open doors for national recognition.

7. Support System: A well-rounded collegiate experience would have been made possible by the university's support system, which included mentorship programs, athletic training staff, and academic support.

8. Fan Base and Community Support: Clark's entire experience may have been improved by the energy of the fan base and the support of the community, which may have added to the atmosphere surrounding basketball games.

9. Future Career Considerations: She may have made her choice based on her expectation of future career opportunities in basketball and elsewhere. Selecting an institution that fits her long-term objectives is essential to a fulfilling college career.

Ultimately, Caitlin Clark probably went through a thorough process when selecting a college, weighing both academic and athletic factors to find the best fit for her future academic and career goals. Her decision surely had a significant impact on how her college basketball career developed.

3:2 Impacts on the team

Beyond her individual accomplishments, Caitlin Clark's influence on her college basketball team has been significant, helping to shape the group's dynamics and overall success. Key facets of her influence are as follows:

1. Offensive Catalyst: Clark is a major offensive catalyst for the team because of her ability to score points. Her ability to put points on the board and create scoring opportunities improves the performance of the team as a whole.

2. Assists and Playmaking: Clark is an accomplished playmaker whose passing and court vision greatly enhance the team's offensive flow. Her assists produce an

offensive strategy that is more dynamic and unpredictable.

3. Leadership both on and off the Court: Clark demonstrates leadership abilities that go beyond his statistical accomplishments. Her influence both on and off the court helps to create a cohesive and winning mindset within the team.

4. Exclusive Demonstrations: Clark shines when it comes to giving clutch performances in tight spots and under pressure. Her teammates are inspired with confidence by her poise and performance in pivotal game situations.

5. Impact on Team Morale: Clark set the bar high for the team with his commitment and work ethic. Her dedication to quality work and never-ending search for development inspires colleagues to raise their own game.

6. Adaptability and Versatility: The team can adjust to different game situations thanks to Clark's versatility.

Caitlin clark

Her versatile skill set gives flexibility to the team's playmaking whether she's scoring, setting up, or playing defense.

7. Drawing Defensive Attention: Clark is frequently the target of intense defensive attention from opposing teams, which opens up opportunities for her teammates. Her influence on team dynamics is demonstrated by the space and scoring opportunities she creates for others.

8. Contribution to Team Success: Clark's individual efforts have a significant impact on the team's overall performance. Her contributions to crucial games are frequently correlated with the team's wins, highlighting her importance as a key component of the winning formula.

9. Influence on Team Chemistry: Clark has a favorable impact on the development of team chemistry. A cohesive and unified team is a result of her ability to build supportive environments and establish connections with teammates.

Caitlin clark

Beyond the scoreboard, Caitlin Clark's influence on the team is evident in her leadership qualities and capacity to improve the team's performance in addition to her physical prowess. Her presence has surely had a lasting impact on the success and culture of the team.

CHAPTER 4: NOTABLE ACHIEVEMENTS

Throughout her basketball career, Caitlin Clark has accumulated a number of noteworthy accomplishments that demonstrate her extraordinary talent and influence on the game. Here are a few of her greatest achievements:

1. High School Accolades: She was recognized as one of the best players in the country and received multiple Player of the Year awards at the high school level.
   - All-State recognition and awards for her exceptional performances in high school contests.

2. College Awards and Recognitions: Her excellence within her collegiate conference was highlighted by her consistent selection to All-Conference teams.
   - A chance to win important national honors, demonstrating her status as one of the best players in women's college basketball.

Caitlin clark

3. Scoring Records: She demonstrated her prolific scoring ability by setting and breaking scoring records at the high school and collegiate levels.
   - Set personal bests for points scored in games, making a big impact on her team's victory.

4. Triple-Doubles: Recorded impressive triple-doubles, displaying her versatility in one-game performances as she thrived in playmaking, rebounding, and scoring.

5. National Recognition: Consistently appearing in national rankings, highlighting her position as one of the best players in college basketball for women.
   - Increased her visibility and recognition by competing for her college and team in major national competitions.

6. Significant Postseason Performances: Played a key role in leading her team to successful postseason runs, particularly in NCAA March Madness and conference tournaments.

Caitlin clark

- Acknowledged for her clutch efforts in pivotal postseason games.

7. Community Engagement: Recognition of her off-court accomplishments, such as her participation in charitable endeavors and the community.
 - Exhibited leadership by making a good influence outside of the basketball court with her platform.

8. Achieved All-American status, securing her position as one of the top players in women's college basketball.
 - Acknowledgment for her exceptional contributions to basketball from a number of basketball publications and organizations.

The noteworthy accomplishments of Caitlin Clark demonstrate not only her unique talent but also her significant influence on the groups she has played for. Her journey from high school stardom to collegiate success has been characterized by an unwavering dedication to excellence and an ever-evolving legacy.

Caitlin clark

4:1 Awards

Throughout her basketball career, Caitlin Clark has received numerous accolades and awards that attest to her exceptional contributions to the game. These are some typical categories of recognition she might have gotten, though the exact ones would change depending on her collegiate seasons and accomplishments:

1. All-Conference Selections: Acknowledgment for her outstanding play in her college conference, frequently securing a spot on All-Conference teams.

2. All-American Honors: She was selected to multiple All-American teams, confirming her place among the best players in women's college basketball.

3. Player of the Year Awards: Honors like Conference Player of the Year, which acknowledges her as the best player in her college association.

Caitlin clark

4. Freshman of the Year: She might be named Freshman of the Year, emphasizing her instant influence in her first collegiate season.

5. Position-Specific Awards: Awards that honor her superiority in particular areas of the game, like best playmaker, top scorer, or exceptional defensive player.

6. National Awards Consideration: A chance to be considered for esteemed national honors like the John R. Wooden Award or the Naismith College Player of the Year.

7. Academic Honors: Acknowledgment for her contributions in the classroom, possibly resulting in selection to the Academic All-American or Academic All-Conference teams.

8. Tournament MVP: She may be eligible to win Tournament MVP if she significantly contributed to her team's victories during the tournament.

9. Community Service Awards: Recognition of her charitable and community service efforts off the court.

10. Sportswoman of the Year: Acknowledged for her leadership, sportsmanship, and good impact both on and off the court.

Together, these honors demonstrate Caitlin Clark's exceptional all-around performance, which includes both her community service and athletic accomplishments. Every honor she has received is proof of her influence on basketball and her commitment to excellence throughout her collegiate career.

4:2 Recognitions

Caitlin Clark has received a great deal of praise and recognition for her exceptional on-court performances. These are a few of the noteworthy honors she had won up until then:

Caitlin clark

1. High School Accomplishments: Winner of the Iowa Gatorade Player Award.
   - Iowa Miss Basketball multiple times, honoring the best high school player in the state.
   - Breaking state records for points in a season and career points.

2. Collegiate Honors: Multiple Big Ten Player and Freshman of the Week recognitions.
   - Selection to the All-Big Ten First Team and the Freshman of the Year award.

3. NCAA All-American Honors: Receiving multiple organizations' All-American honors, demonstrating her influence on the national scene.

4. USBWA National Freshman of the Year: Awarded the title of National Freshman of the Year by the U.S. Basketball Writers Association (USBWA).

Caitlin clark

5. John R. Wooden Award Finalist: Selected as one of the finalists for the esteemed John R. Wooden Award, which recognizes the best college basketball player.

6. Naismith Trophy Finalist: The recognition as a Naismith College Player of the Year Award finalist.

7. Wade Trophy Finalist: Acknowledgment as a finalist for the Wade Trophy, which is given to the top NCAA player for women's basketball.

8. AP All-American: Demonstrating her national standing by earning a spot on the Associated Press (AP) All-American Team.

9. ESPNW National Player of the Year Finalist: Being a finalist for the prestigious award that honors excellence in women's college basketball, the ESPNW National Player of the Year.

10. Big Ten Tournament Success: She made a significant contribution to her team's victory and received

Caitlin clark

recognition for her outstanding performances in the Big Ten Tournament.

CHAPTER 5: PLAYING STYLE AND SKILLS

A variety of dynamic skills define Caitlin Clark's playing style, which makes her an incredible force on the basketball court. The following are salient features of her technique and abilities:

1. Scoring Prowess: Clark's remarkable scoring ability is well-known. She routinely scores a high number of points whether she is shooting mid-range, driving to the hoop, or beyond the arc.

2. Vision and Passing of the Court: Clark is an excellent passer with great court vision and playmaking skills. Her ability to create opportunities for her teammates through playmaking is just as important as her scoring total.

Caitlin clark

3. Ball handling: Clark's strong ball handling abilities enable him to get past defenses, take down opponents off the dribble, and dictate the game's pace.

Shooting Range: Skillful at making shots at a variety of ranges, including three-pointers. Because of her long shooting range, she can score from anywhere, which forces opponents to extend and opens up space for her teammates.

5. Versatility: One of Clark's greatest strengths as a player is her versatility. She is a versatile player who can switch between scoring, facilitating, and rebounding depending on what the team needs.

6. Decision-Making: Her efficacy on the court is enhanced by her strong decision-making abilities. Clark's basketball IQ is an important asset when it comes to making decisions about when to drive, when to take a shot, or when to pass the ball.

Caitlin clark

7. Clutch Performances: Exhibits poise and delivers when it matters most. Clark is a dependable go-to player for her team because of her capacity to perform well under duress.

8. Rebounding: Clark makes a major contribution to rebounding even though her main position is guard. Her perseverance on the boards gives her a different aspect to play and helps the team win as a whole.

9. Defensive Intensity: Clark is a known offensive player, but she also brings a strong defensive game to the table. She can press opponents and obstruct passing lanes, which gives her skill set a defensive element.

10. Leadership Qualities: Clark possesses leadership traits that are evident on the court in addition to his individual talents. She fosters team cohesiveness by inspiring teammates, speaking clearly, and setting a good example.

Caitlin clark

Caitlin Clark is a formidable force in women's college basketball thanks to her playing style and skill set, which display a well-rounded and dynamic athlete. Her capacity to influence different aspects of the game helps the teams she plays for and herself succeed as a whole in addition to herself.

5:1 Offensive prowess

One of the most distinctive qualities of Caitlin Clark's basketball skill set is her offensive ability, which makes her one of the most prolific scorers in the league. Her offensive prowess is largely attributed to the following factors:

1. Shooting Accuracy: Clark has a remarkable touch when it comes to shooting, whether it's in the paint, mid-range, or beyond the arc. She is a continual threat to score because of her accuracy and reliability.

Caitlin clark

2. Three-Point Range Acquisition: Her ability to score from beyond the three-point line is one of her most notable offensive qualities. When Clark connects on a long-range shot, defenses are forced to extend, making room for Clark and her teammates.

3. Variety of Scoring: Clark is a skilled scorer who can succeed with jump shots, layups, floaters, and pull-up jumpers. Her wide range of scoring styles makes her challenging to defend.

4. Finishing at the Rim: Clark's quickness and rim-finishing skills enable her to get past defenses and make challenging layups. Her offensive game is enhanced by the inventiveness with which she finishes plays at the hoop.

5. Free Throw Proficiency: Clark makes effective use of his free throw line and scores when he gets the ball in the charity stripe. Her team's score is enhanced by her ability to reliably convert free throws.

Caitlin clark

6. Playmaking Techniques: Clark is best known for his scoring, but he also makes plays that greatly enhance the offensive flow. She can influence the game in ways other than just scoring goals because of her vision and passing prowess, which open up scoring opportunities for teammates.

7. Transition Offense: Clark thrives in transition, taking advantage of quick breaks. She is a constant threat in fast-paced offensive situations because of her speed, ball handling skills, and open-court decision-making.

8. High Basketball IQ: She can read defenses, take advantage of mismatches, and make wise decisions to maximize offensive efficiency because of her high basketball IQ.

9. Off-Ball Movement: Clark can find open spots for shots by separating from defenders with effective off-ball movement. Her proficiency with screen navigation and spacing plays a part in her high score.

10. Clutch Performances: In clutch circumstances, Clark's offensive ability is especially apparent. Her confidence and dependability as a go-to scorer are demonstrated by her ability to step up and make clutch baskets under duress.

Caitlin Clark is an offensive weapon because of her versatility and efficiency on the court in addition to her sheer volume of points scored. She is a player who consistently draws defensive attention due to her varied offensive style and is essential to her team's success.

5:2 Defensive abilities

Although Caitlin Clark's offensive skills garner most of the attention, her defensive skills also play a part in her overall impact on the basketball court. She plays the following defensive strategies:

Caitlin clark

1. Perimeter Defense: Clark can effectively defend opponents on the perimeter thanks to her quickness and agility. Their ability to drive to the basket and create open shots is hindered by her ability to stay on top of her assignment.

2. Steals and Deflections: She can produce steals and deflections since she has an active pair of hands. Clark induces turnovers and blocks passing lanes with his anticipatory and fast reactions.

3. Ball Pressure: Uses strong ball pressure to make it difficult for opponents to easily carry out their offensive plays. Because of her persistence on the ball, opponents may make snap judgments.

4. Transition Defense: Clark is an offensive player, but he also shows that he can quickly switch back to defense in a fast-break scenario. Her dedication to transition defense hinders the opposition team's ability to score easily.

Caitlin clark

5. Rebounding Defensively: Clark isn't your typical post player, but he does help with defensive rebounding. Her ability to grab rebounds aids in reducing opponents' second-chance opportunities.

6. Versatility in Defensive Assignments: Clark can guard several positions due to her defensive versatility. Her team's adaptability gives them a tactical edge and facilitates productive matchups with various opponents.

7. Defensive Communication: Engages in active communication with teammates to help plan defensive rotations, switches, and overall strategies. She is a capable leader on both ends of the court.

8. Defensive Awareness: Reads offensive plays and rotates in a timely manner, displaying a high degree of defensive awareness. Clark's proficiency with the game enhances her ability to defend.

9. Drawing Charges: Shows that she is prepared to offer her body as a sacrifice. This unselfish deed could turn the tide in her team's favor and result in turnovers.

10. Adaptability: Modifies her defensive strategy according to the opponent and state of the game. Clark modifies her playmaking style according to the situation, whether she is playing tight man-to-man defense or help defense.

Despite the fact that she may be best on offense, Caitlin Clark's defensive efforts demonstrate her dedication to being a well-rounded player. Her total effect on the basketball court is influenced by both her strong offensive play and her defensive efforts.

5:3 Leadership on the Court

One of the most distinctive aspects of Caitlin Clark's basketball persona is her leadership on the court, which

Caitlin clark

affects both her own play and the team's overall success. Key components of her leadership style are as follows:

1. Lead by Example: Clark sets the bar high for her teammates by playing at a high level every time and exhibiting the diligence and work ethic that are expected of her.

2. Vocal Leadership: Engages in active communication with teammates on the court, offering direction, calling plays, and building team spirit. Clark's outspoken demeanor contributes to the cohesive team dynamic.

3. Motivational Skills: She uses her words and deeds to inspire and motivate her teammates. Clark's ability to motivate others is beneficial for the team environment, whether it is on the court, in the locker room, or during timeouts.

When the team needs it most, the player who demonstrates leadership in pivotal situations steps up and gives clutch performances. Her capacity to perform well under duress sets an example for her colleagues.

5. Emotional Intelligence: Demonstrates emotional intelligence by comprehending the dynamics within her team and reacting suitably to various circumstances. Fostering a positive team environment is facilitated by Clark's ability to read and encourage teammates.

6. Supporting Colleagues: Recognizes and celebrates teammates' accomplishments while actively offering support and encouragement. One of Clark's leadership responsibilities is fostering a culture of respect and unity among team members.

7. Adaptability: Modifies her leadership approach based on the requirements of the group. Clark modifies her style for optimal impact, whether she's working with more seasoned teammates or mentoring younger players.

8. Work Ethic: Establishes a rigorous code of conduct for work ethic in both games and practice. It is her

teammates' constant drive for improvement that inspires Clark to perform at a higher level.

9. Resilience and Positivity: Retains a positive outlook despite obstacles, exhibiting resilience and boosting her teammates' self-assurance. Clark's disposition supports a strong team spirit.

10. Inclusive Leadership: Guarantees that each team member experiences a sense of worth and belonging. A sense of belonging is fostered by Clark's inclusive leadership, which improves team cohesion overall.

Beyond just her individual abilities, Caitlin Clark's leadership on the court also includes her capacity to uplift, encourage, and inspire her team's overall performance. The success and positive culture of the teams she leads are greatly enhanced by her presence as a leader.

CHAPTER 6: CHALLENGE

Caitlin Clark has had a great deal of success in her basketball career, but she probably had difficulties too. Among the possible challenges she might have faced are:

1. High Expectations: It could be difficult to live up to the pressure and expectations that come with being a highly regarded player from high school into college. Whether you meet or surpass these standards, more scrutiny may follow.

2. College Play Adaptation: There can be difficulties when moving from high school basketball to collegiate basketball. The first obstacles might have been getting used to a new squad and coaching philosophy as well as adjusting to a faster and more physical style of play.

3. Defensive Tactics: To lessen Clark's influence on the game, opponents may use particular defensive tactics. A

variety of defensive schemes, aggressive defense, and double teams could provide difficulties that call for tactical changes.

4. Physical Toll and Injury: It can be difficult to manage injuries or the physical strain of a rigorous schedule, just like for any athlete. For long-term success, performance and physical health must be balanced.

5. Group Dynamics: Developing positive team dynamics can be difficult, particularly if you're a standout player. Success requires navigating team dynamics, recognizing teammates' playing styles, and encouraging cooperation.

6. Academic Demands: It can be difficult to juggle the demands of a college athlete's demanding schedule with the obligations of academics. Effective time management is a common challenge for athletes and academics alike.

7. Aspirations from Media and Fans: It can be difficult to handle the attention and expectations that come from the public, media, and fans. The ability to remain composed

and focused in the face of external pressure is something that elite athletes must master.

8. Difficulties and Losses: It can be emotionally taxing to suffer losses or setbacks, whether they relate to one's own performance or the success of the team. The ability to overcome hardship is a critical component of mental toughness in athletes.

9. Leadership Accountabilities: Although it can be a strength, leadership can also present difficulties. It takes tact to balance the obligations of being a leader on and off the court, especially in trying circumstances.

10. Deciding in the Future: Making decisions regarding one's future, including possible professional opportunities and post-college career paths, can be difficult for a prominent athlete. Making choices that support both professional and personal objectives is a continuous process.

Caitlin clark

It's critical to remember that conquering obstacles is a natural part of the athletic journey and promotes development on and off the court. Caitlin Clark's overall success in the basketball world is probably influenced by her ability to overcome these obstacles.

6:1 Triumphs

Caitlin Clark's basketball career has been filled with victories, which attest to her tenacity, talent, and capacity to overcome obstacles. Among her career's noteworthy victories could be:

1. Excellent High School Career: Clark had a successful high school career, winning several Player of the Year honors and being named among the country's best high school athletes.

2. College Recruitment Success: It's a victory in and of itself that she was able to navigate the cutthroat college recruitment process and select a program that fits her

goals. Her choice probably had a role in her later success as a collegiate basketball player.

3. Impressive First Season: It is a noteworthy accomplishment for her to make an early impression during her collegiate debut. Her ability and adaptability are highlighted by her success in a novel and demanding setting.

4. Setting Scoring Records: Clark's offensive prowess is demonstrated by breaking scoring records at the high school and collegiate levels. Establishing standards for personal success is a victory with enduring significance.

5. All-American Honors: Her continuous excellence on the court is demonstrated by her receipt of All-American honors. One of her biggest victories as a college player is being regarded as one of the best players in the country.

6. Acknowledgment for Leadership: It is a victory to be acknowledged for her leadership both on and off the court. Clark's capacity to inspire her teammates and set a

Caitlin clark

good example for the group helps foster a successful team environment.

7. Postseason Success: Postseason victories, like notable showings in conference tournaments or major contributions during NCAA March Madness, add to her overall influence and the team's accomplishments.

8. National Exposure and Accolades: Her achievements as one of the best players in women's college basketball are confirmed by her national recognition and awards from numerous basketball publications and organizations.

9. Impact and Community Engagement: It is a victory to use philanthropy and community engagement to make a positive difference outside of the basketball court. Utilizing her position to uplift and support the neighborhood is indicative of her wider impact.

10. Personal Growth and Development: Throughout her journey, she has consistently grown and developed as an

athlete and a person, which represents victories. Her continued success can be attributed to her ability to overcome obstacles, adjust to new situations, and develop as a player.

Caitlin Clark's victories show off not just her personal accomplishments but also her role in the team's success and her wider influence in the basketball community. A string of successes along the way have molded her into an exceptional athlete and leader in her sport.

6:2 Overcoming Adversity

Although Caitlin Clark's personal struggles may not be widely known, obstacles and disappointments are a common part of the journey for athletes. Athletes who overcome adversity are resilient and determined individuals. Here are a few common strategies that athletes, like Clark, can use to overcome hardship:

Caitlin clark

1. Mental Toughness: When confronted with obstacles, cultivating mental toughness is essential. This entails remaining focused, remaining upbeat, and possessing the mental toughness to endure adversity.

2. Growing from Failures: Adversity can be overcome by athletes by viewing setbacks as opportunities for learning and growth. Examining obstacles enables the growth of one's abilities and self, which promotes long-term achievement.

3. Adaptability: Unexpected changes or obstacles are a common occurrence for athletes. One essential component of conquering obstacles is being flexible and willing to modify tactics or methods when faced with difficulty.

4. Strong Support System: Having a solid support network, which consists of teammates, coaches, family, and friends, helps motivate and emotionally support an athlete through trying times. Consulting with others for advice and support can be very helpful.

5. Goal Setting: Athletes can maintain focus and motivation by creating clear, attainable short- and long-term goals. Overcoming adversity involves achieving small goals along the way to recovery or improvement.

6. Professional Advice: Consulting with mentors, coaches, or sports psychologists can be helpful. Experts can offer advice on how to handle stress, improve mental toughness, and deal with hardship.

7. Physical Rehabilitation: Adhering to a comprehensive and regimented rehabilitation program is crucial in situations involving physical hardship, such as injuries. The process of returning to peak performance gradually involves physical recovery.

8. Self-Reflection: Athletes can better understand their strengths, shortcomings, and areas for growth by reflecting on themselves. Developing coping skills and

resilience can be facilitated by having a good understanding of oneself.

9. Maintaining Perspective: Athletes can stay balanced by keeping an eye beyond the current obstacles. A positive outlook can be fostered by acknowledging that obstacles are a part of the journey and that setbacks are temporary.

10. Coherent Work Culture: It's critical to keep up a constant work ethic even in difficult circumstances. Persistently putting in effort to improve and stay dedicated to training helps people overcome adversity.

Although Caitlin Clark's exact struggles aren't discussed here, athletes of her caliber frequently show resiliency and the capacity to overcome obstacles, which helps them succeed in their respective sports over the long run.

Caitlin clark

6:3 Memorable Games and Moments

Exciting games and moments involving Caitlin Clark abound. The following are the kinds of incidents that frequently stick in the memory of a brilliant basketball player:

1. Record-Breaking Performances: Clark's games that culminate in new scoring records or noteworthy statistical milestones tend to be especially unforgettable. Setting records in high school or college enhances a player's legacy.

2. Clutch Shots and Game-Winners: Clark's clutch plays, particularly those that win games, leave an indelible impression on fans. The ability to perform under pressure demonstrates a player's poise and talent.

3. Notable Postseason Achievements: Postseason tournaments are often the scene of memorable games.

Caitlin clark

Outstanding performances that propel her team to victories in NCAA March Madness or conference tournaments would be noteworthy.

4. Triple-Doubles: Clark's all-around abilities are on display in games where she records triple-doubles, or double digits in points, rebounds, and assists. These are exceptional and uncommon in a player's career.

5. Wins Against Top-Ranked Teams: Wins against rival teams or opponents with high rankings are frequently noteworthy. Bringing her team to victories in difficult matches adds to Clark's legacy.

6. Career-High Scoring Games: Clark's scoring prowess is demonstrated in games where she reaches her career-high point total. These spectacular performances frequently end up being remembered as highlights.

7. National Recognition and Awards: The story of Clark's basketball career is enhanced by the times she is

recognized nationally, such as when she is named an All-American or wins prestigious awards.

8. Community Engagement and Impactful Off-Court Moments: Outside of the court, noteworthy events could involve philanthropic work, community involvement, or using her platform to further good deeds.

9. Emotional and Inspirational Moments: Fans and the basketball community can be deeply affected by games or moments in which Clark shows genuine emotion, triumphs over hardship, or inspires others.

10. Farewell or Senior Night Moments: Whether it's a farewell game or senior night, the end of a collegiate career can be an emotional and unforgettable moment for the player and the supporters.

CHAPTER 7: OFF THE COURT

Even though Caitlin Clark is well-known for her accomplishments on the court, her hobbies and extracurricular pursuits help to paint a complete picture of her character. Even though her off-court activities may not have been well-documented, athletes frequently partake in the following activities outside of their sport:

1. Studies and Interests: A student-athlete's life must include juggling academics and athletics. It's likely that Caitlin Clark studies hard and strives for academic success in addition to her basketball responsibilities.

2. Community Involvement: Athletes frequently take part in charitable endeavors and volunteer work in their communities. Clark might take part in charitable endeavors, lending her support to causes close to her heart and having a beneficial influence off the court.

Caitlin clark

3. Social Media Presence: Athletes frequently utilize social media sites to interact with followers, divulge personal details, and advocate for different causes. Clark might use social media to discuss some of her hobbies and experiences outside of the court.

4. Interests and Hobbies: Outside of their sport, athletes have a wide range of interests and pastimes. It's possible that Clark engages in hobbies or interests outside of music, art, reading, or other leisure activities that enhance her general wellbeing.

5. Leadership and Mentorship: Athletes frequently participate in leadership positions or mentorship initiatives off the court. Clark might take part in community leadership programs, mentor younger players, or impart wisdom to aspiring athletes.

6. Health and Wellness: It's critical for athletes to maintain both their physical and mental health. Clark might partake in mindfulness exercises, physical training, or other wellness-oriented pursuits.

Caitlin clark

7. Education and Skill Development: Opportunities for both professional and personal growth are frequently sought after by athletes. Clark could spend time attending seminars, training sessions, or classes to broaden her knowledge and skill set outside of basketball.

8. Travel and Exploration: Due to the demands of collegiate athletics, athletes may be able to take part in tournaments, games, or other events that require travel. Through these encounters, Clark might travel and experience different cultures.

9. Personal Relationships: An athlete's life revolves around forming and preserving bonds with friends, family, and teammates. Clark probably enjoys spending time with his teammates and loved ones off the court.

10. Future Career Considerations: Athletes frequently think about their careers after sports. Clark might be looking into possible educational programs, internships,

Caitlin clark

or career routes that fit with her interests outside of basketball.

Although these are broad strokes, Caitlin Clark's off-court details are private to her and might not be widely reported. You might want to check her official social media accounts, as well as any interviews or features that offer insights into her life outside of basketball, for the most recent information on her off-court activities.

7:1 Academic pursuits

Student-athletes usually manage to juggle their demanding athletic schedules with their academic obligations. For student-athletes like Caitlin Clark, the following general factors should be taken into account when pursuing academic goals:

1. Collegiate Studies: Caitlin Clark is probably enrolled in a particular academic program at her college because

she is a student-athlete. She can choose a major or academic focus that reflects her interests outside of basketball as well as her professional aspirations.

2. Academic Achievement: A lot of student-athletes place equal importance on their academic and athletic accomplishments. Maintaining a specific GPA and actively participating in coursework are two examples of academic achievement.

3. Managing Commitments: Juggling the rigors of academics and athletics can be difficult. Student-athletes must possess strong organizational and time management abilities to succeed in both fields.

4. Support Services: Academic advising, tutoring, and study materials are just a few of the support services that colleges frequently offer to student-athletes. Clark could use these resources to improve her academic standing.

5. Future Career Goals: Academic pursuits are frequently weighed against future career aspirations for

Caitlin clark

student-athletes. Clark's choice of major and coursework may be influenced by particular interests or career goals.

6. Leadership in Academic Settings: A number of student-athletes take on active leadership roles in academic environments. This could entail taking part in mentorship programs, academic associations, or other endeavors.

7. Athletes and Community Engagement through Academics: Athletes can also engage with the community through their academic endeavors. Participation in initiatives or programs for educational outreach may contribute to their overall impact.

8. Professional Development: Student-athletes may look for opportunities for professional development outside of the classroom. This could entail conferences, workshops, or internships associated with their areas of academic interest.

Caitlin clark

7:2 Community involvement

Many athletes participate in a variety of community-related activities, including student-athletes like Clark. Athletes frequently engage in the following general ways in their communities:

1. Youth Sports Programs: Athletes can support or take part in these programs, offering young athletes guidance, inspiration, and mentoring.

2. Basketball Clinics and Camps: One popular method for athletes to impart their knowledge and skills to aspiring players is by organizing or taking part in basketball clinics and camps.

3. Charitable Initiatives: Athletes frequently participate in charitable endeavors, giving their time or money to support causes that they fervently believe in. This could be going out to raise money, running campaigns to raise awareness, or volunteering directly for nonprofits.

4. School and Education Outreach: In order to promote academic success, athletes frequently interact with schools and other educational establishments by taking part in reading programs, motivational speeches, and other events.

5. Community Events and Festivals: Athletes can build relationships with locals and enhance the vibrancy of their communities by taking part in parades, festivals, and other community events.

Athletes have the opportunity to endorse health and wellness programs that enhance physical fitness, nutrition education, and general well-being within their communities.

7. Actions to Stop Bullying: Some athletes support the cause of standing up to bullying. To address this crucial issue, they might visit schools or take part in anti-bullying campaigns.

Caitlin clark

8. Hospital and Health Facility Visits: Athletes frequently go to hospitals and health centers to spend time with patients, offer support, and spread awareness of different health-related issues.

9. Support for Veterans and the Military: Many athletes support the causes of veterans and active military personnel. Engagement could take the form of awareness-raising campaigns, veteran support programs, or tours of military installations.

10. Environmental Initiatives: Athletes have the opportunity to promote sustainability and environmental conservation. This could be taking part in clean-up campaigns, planting trees, or contributing to environmentally beneficial projects.

Caitlin clark

CHAPTER 8: LEGACY

Basketball player Caitlin Clark is renowned for her extraordinary abilities and accomplishments in the game. Athlete legacy is a dynamic term that includes an athlete's influence on their sport, community, and next generation. Although specifics regarding Caitlin Clark's legacy might have changed since my last post, the following factors could have an impact on an athlete's legacy:

1. Achievements and Records: A player's legacy is shaped by his or her ability to break and set records in both high school and collegiate basketball. Caitlin Clark's basketball legacy will probably include her scoring records and individual honors.

2. Impact on Teams: A player's legacy is shaped by the impact they have on their teams' achievements. Clark's legacy is shaped in part by her leadership, her

contributions to team victories, and her influence on the general performance of her teams.

3. Community Engagement: Athletes who make a positive impact on their communities through active engagement do so. As part of her wider influence, Clark's participation in outreach, community service, and charitable endeavors may be recalled.

4. Role as a Leader: An athlete's legacy is shaped by their leadership abilities both on and off the court. In the basketball community, Caitlin Clark's leadership qualities will be ingrained in the basketball community's memory.

5. Sportsmanship and Character: An athlete's legacy is greatly influenced by their demonstration of sportsmanship, integrity, and character. People's opinions of Clark as an athlete and person are shaped by the way she handles herself in wins and losses.

6. Inspiration to Others: Sportspeople who motivate others, particularly the upcoming generation of athletes, leave a lasting impression. A significant part of Clark's overall legacy is the influence she has had as an inspiration and role model for young basketball players.

7. Recognition from the Media and Fans: Caitlin Clark's legacy may be impacted by how the public views her and how the media portrays her. Positive media attention, fan adoration, and support are all factors that shape an athlete's legacy.

8. Contributions to the Game: Players who make a significant impact on the development of their sport leave a long-lasting legacy. This could involve advocating for beneficial changes in the sport or introducing novel tactics or playing styles.

9. Alumni and College Legacy: Caitlin Clark leaves a lasting impression on the college basketball scene due to her influence on the program, her relationships with

coaches and teammates, and her overall impact as an alumna.

10. Long-Term Impact Outside Basketball: Sportsmen and women who have a positive influence outside of basketball, such as in business, advocacy, or other domains, leave a more lasting and extensive legacy.

As Caitlin Clark plays more basketball and participates in more activities both on and off the court, her legacy will only grow.

8:1 Impacts

Caitlin Clark's contributions to her basketball career and beyond have been substantial in a number of areas. The following are possible effects she could have had:

1. On-Court Dominance: The success of Clark's high school and collegiate basketball teams is directly related to her extraordinary abilities and performances on the

Caitlin clark

court. Her leadership, playmaking skills, and scoring prowess help the team win and accomplish goals.

2. Records and Achievements: Clark's impact in the area of individual accomplishments is aided by his setting of scoring records and his receipt of prestigious awards. Her accomplishments demonstrate that she is one of the best players in women's collegiate basketball.

3. Team Success: Clark's contributions and leadership have probably been a major factor in her teams' achievements. Her influence goes beyond individual honors to include team accomplishments like conference championships, tournament wins, and postseason runs.

4. Community Engagement: Clark's influence extends outside the courtroom if he participates in community projects. Engaging in the community, whether through outreach initiatives, mentoring, or charitable work, can have a positive impact on the lives of people she comes into contact with.

Caitlin clark

5. Affect on Young Sportspeople: Being a well-known athlete, Clark's accomplishments can motivate and have an impact on budding basketball players. She might inspire the following generation to strive for their academic and athletic aspirations.

6. Enhancing Women's Basketball: Prominent athletes like Clark help to make women's basketball more visible and well-liked. Their influence goes beyond their own accomplishments; they contribute to improving women's sports' general standing and level of recognition.

7. Media and Marketing Impact: High-profile athletes have the power to influence how women's basketball is portrayed in the media and promoted. Because of Clark's success, women in sports media may have more opportunities and visibility.

8. Alumni Impact: Clark's tenure in her college program adds to the history of the basketball program at the university. Her influence as an alumna could sway

potential participants, enhancing the program's continued success.

9. Leadership Impact: Clark has an impact on the dynamics and culture of the team if she is acknowledged for her leadership abilities. Coworkers and the program's general atmosphere can be positively impacted for a long time by leadership, both on and off the court.

10. Broader Social Impact: By addressing social issues, supporting positive change, and using their influence to contribute to societal discussions, athletes, especially those with a significant platform, can have a broader social impact.

8:2 Women's Basketball Contributions

Caitlin Clark has had a significant impact on women's basketball through her leadership, exceptional play, and influence on the game.

Caitlin clark

1. On-Court Excellence: The general thrill and competitiveness of women's basketball have been enhanced by Clark's extraordinary talents, scoring prowess, and playmaking on the court. Her accomplishments demonstrate the great caliber of talent in the field.

2. Improving Women's Basketball's Visibility: Being a well-known player, Clark helps to increase women's basketball's awareness and respect. Her accomplishments and performances command attention, drawing supporters and media interest in the women's game.

3. Setting Scoring Records: Clark's ability to score points, which includes breaking records in high school and college, exemplifies women's basketball's offensive talent. These kinds of accomplishments help dispel misconceptions and highlight the talent of female athletes.

Caitlin clark

4. Inspiring Future Generations: Young female basketball players who aspire to be like Clark find inspiration in her. Her on-court accomplishments inspire the following generation to follow their sporting aspirations, which has a positive effect on the expansion of women's basketball.

5. Status of Leadership and Role Modeling: If Clark is acknowledged for her leadership abilities, her influence extends beyond her personal accomplishments. In addition to being a great role model for upcoming athletes, she helps to develop a leadership and sportsmanship culture in women's sports.

6. Contributions to Collegiate Basketball: The thrill of NCAA women's basketball is enhanced by Clark's collegiate basketball performances. Her influence on the college basketball program and her involvement in prestigious competitions add to the popularity and success of women's college basketball as a whole.

Caitlin clark

7. Promoting Women in Athletics: Prominent sportsmen frequently add to the larger discussion about gender parity in athletics. Clark might make use of her position to promote fairness, acknowledgement, and assistance for female athletes and basketball players.

8. Media and Marketing Impact: Players with a lot of media exposure, like Clark, help to promote and brand women's basketball. The sport's general growth and perception are influenced by increased visibility and positive representation in the media.

9. Involvement with Women's Basketball Community: Clark promotes a sense of unity and connection through his interactions with teammates, fans, and the larger women's basketball community. Social media engagement and in-person interactions with fans foster an active and supportive fan base.

10. The History of Women's College Basketball: Clark adds to the heritage and past of women's collegiate basketball if she has had a noteworthy influence on her

school's program. Her accomplishments are woven into the story of collegiate athletics.

8:3 Influence on Future Generations

Caitlin Clark will have a lasting and profound impact on future generations, especially in the area of women's basketball. She can influence and mold young athletes' dreams in the following ways:

1. Skill and Talent Showcase: Clark's extraordinary basketball skills and talent act as a showcase for aspiring players, showing them the possibilities and successes that can be attained with commitment and hard work.

2. Breaking Stereotypes: Clark challenges preconceived ideas about the abilities of female athletes and breaks stereotypes by succeeding in a traditionally male-dominated sport. This opens the door to a future in sports that is more equal and inclusive.

Caitlin clark

3. Workplace Ethics and Commitment: Young athletes look up to Clark because of her remarkable work ethic and devotion to the sport, which exemplifies the commitment needed to compete at the highest levels. Her experience serves as a reminder of the value of tenacity and ongoing development.

4. Sportsmanship and Leadership: If Clark is acknowledged for her leadership abilities and sportsmanship, she becomes an inspiration for traits other than athletic ability. She is a role model for young athletes, showing them how to lead with integrity and respect both on and off the court.

5. Academic and Athletic Balances: As a student-athlete, Clark's capacity to strike a balance between rigorous academics and competitive sports can serve as an example for young athletes, encouraging them to give their education equal weight with their love of sports.

6. Representation Matters: Young girls who want to play collegiate or professional basketball can find role models

in Clark's prominence in women's basketball. Her example of a successful female athlete gives other girls hope that they, too, can fulfill their sporting ambitions.

7. Advocacy for Gender Equality: By promoting gender equality in sports, Clark can encourage young athletes to fight for fair treatment and equal opportunities in their athletic endeavors.

8. Community Engagement and Philanthropy: Young athletes learn the value of giving back and using their platform to positively impact the community through any involvement in community engagement or philanthropic activities.

9. Mentorship and Advice: Due to her success, Clark may decide to mentor young athletes, providing them with advice and support as they navigate their own athletic journeys. Personal accounts of struggles and victories have a special power.

Caitlin clark

10. Equating Aspirations: Clark demonstrates the significance of striking a balance between one's own goals and the cooperative nature of team sports by overseeing both individual accomplishments and team successes. Young athletes who are working toward their own objectives may find this lesson useful.

Caitlin Clark's impact on upcoming generations is probably only going to increase as her career develops and she keeps adding to the field of women's basketball. Her influence goes beyond the numbers and awards; she has shaped women's sports and motivated young athletes to dream big and follow their passions with tenacity.

CHAPTER 9: RISING STAR STATUS

The story of Caitlin Clark's ascent to prominence in the basketball world is one of natural talent mixed with perseverance and hard work. Clark was born in Des Moines, Iowa, on June 22, 2001. Her meteoric rise from amateur athlete to rising star is a credit to her extraordinary abilities and her influence on the sport.

Initial Years and the Origins of Basketball:
At an early age, Caitlin's passion for basketball was sparked by the sound of a bouncing ball hitting the driveway. Her early enthusiasm for the game laid the groundwork for an incredible journey.

Stardom in high school:
Clark shot to fame as a standout Dowling Catholic high school student in West Des Moines. She attracted attention and accolades due to her scoring prowess, court vision, and leadership on the court. She had an unquenchable desire for success and constantly gave

Caitlin clark

exceptional performances that highlighted her talent for scoring and setting up plays.

Achievements That Broke Records:
Throughout his high school career, Clark broke numerous records. She made a lasting impression as one of the state's most prolific scorers and etched her name in Iowa high school basketball history by breaking records for points scored at the state level.

Collegiate Success Stories at Iowa:
Clark never stopped shining as she brought her talents to the collegiate level. She adapted to the rigorous world of NCAA Division I basketball with ease while playing for the University of Iowa Hawkeyes. Her influence was immediate, garnering her multiple awards and All-American distinctions.

Outstanding Playmaking and Scoring:
The remarkable ability of Caitlin Clark to score points from anywhere on the court is a defining feature of her style of play. She is a dynamic playmaker who captivates

Caitlin clark

audiences with her electrifying performances and keeps defenders on their toes thanks to her three-point shooting, ball handling abilities, and court awareness.

Both on and off the court, leadership:
In addition to her skill at scoring, Clark took on a leadership role on the court. She gained not only a reputation as a standout player but also as a leader thanks to her capacity to inspire her team, produce clutch plays under duress, and lead by example.

National Acknowledgment and Media Attention:
Caitlin Clark found herself in the national limelight as her star kept rising. Her personality and the impact she was having on the sport of basketball were highlighted along with her basketball skills through interviews and features in the media.

Possibility of Career Achievement:
As Caitlin Clark began her college career, rumors circulated regarding her potential for success in the business world. Her journey was made even more

exciting by the anticipation of her being selected in the WNBA draft, which left both fans and analysts wondering what kind of impact she could have on the professional scene.

Off-Court Influence and Generosity:
Caitlin Clark's reputation as a rising star in basketball went beyond her interactions on the court and into the community. Her growing legacy gained depth from her charitable endeavors and attempts to have a positive influence off the court.

Prospects for the Future and Further Ascent:
Caitlin Clark's status as a rising star is expected to continue to rise as her journey continues. Her influence both on and off the court, along with the possibility of a prosperous professional career, suggest that this young athlete has a path that leads to greatness.

It's critical to acknowledge the intangibles that characterize Caitlin Clark as a player and person in addition to her accomplishments and statistics when

Caitlin clark

describing her status as a rising star. She is regarded as one of basketball's most promising and inspirational figures because of her journey, which is a compelling story that appeals to both fans and aspiring athletes.

CONCLUSION

One of the greatest basketball players ever, Caitlin Clark, takes readers on an inspirational journey through her life and career in "Caitlin Clark: A Shooting Star's Journey—Beyond the Buzzer." Caitlin Clark's journey from her early days of practicing in the driveway to her rise to prominence as a record-breaking collegiate basketball player highlights not only her extraordinary skills on the court but also the tenacity and resolve that characterize her.

Readers experience the highs and lows, victories and setbacks, and unwavering passion that drives Clark forward as the pages turn. This story explores the facets of a multifaceted athlete—her leadership, her influence on the community, and the unwavering spirit that makes her unique—beyond the buzzer-beaters and awards.

Caitlin clark

In addition to games won and records broken, the book delves into the decisions made, the hardships faced, and the personal and athletic development that took place. In addition to becoming a basketball phenomenon, Caitlin Clark also becomes a representation of commitment, good sportsmanship, and the limitless potential that exists in every rising star.

Caitlin Clark's story is a testament to the enduring power of passion, hard work, and the pursuit of excellence as she considers the next chapter in her journey, whether it be on professional courts or in endeavors beyond basketball. "Beyond the Buzzer" perfectly encapsulates the spirit of a young athlete who, like a meteor striking the sky, leaves a lasting impression on both the sport and the hearts of those who follow in her footsteps.

Finally, this book encourages readers to consider the larger significance of Caitlin Clark's journey—a journey that goes beyond the basketball court and shows the greatness that can be within every person who is willing

Caitlin clark

to pursue their goals with unwavering determination. The excitement for what's beyond the buzzer builds as one chapter comes to an end, with promises of new adventures and the shooting star's continuous ascent.

Made in United States
Orlando, FL
08 June 2024

47643169R00057